Look, a Starfish!

by Tessa Kenan

BUMBA BOOKS™

LERNER PUBLICATIONS ◆ MINNEAPOLIS

Note to Educators:

Throughout this book, you'll find critical thinking questions. These can be used to engage young readers in thinking critically about the topic and in using the text and photos to do so.

Lerner Publications Company
A division of Lerner Publishing Group, Inc.
241 First Avenue North
Minneapolis, MN 55401 USA

For reading levels and more information, look up this title at www.lernerbooks.com.

Library of Congress Cataloging-in-Publication Data

Names: Kenan, Tessa, author.
Title: Look, a starfish! / by Tessa Kenan.
Description: Minneapolis : Lerner Publications, [2017] | Series: Bumba books—I see ocean animals | Audience: Age 4–8. | Audience: K to Grade 3. | Includes bibliographical references and index.
Identifiers: LCCN 2016001075 (print) | LCCN 2016003114 (ebook) | ISBN 9781512414233 (lb : alk. paper) | ISBN 9781512415131 (pb : alk. paper) | ISBN 9781512415148 (eb pdf)
Subjects: LCSH: Starfishes—Juvenile literature.
Classification: LCC QL384.A8 K45 2017 (print) | LCC QL384.A8 (ebook) | DDC 593.9/3—dc23

LC record available at http://lccn.loc.gov/2016001075

Manufactured in the United States of America
1 – VP – 7/15/16

LERNER e SOURCE

Expand learning beyond the printed book. Download free, complementary educational resources for this book from our website, www.lerneresource.com.

Table of
Contents

Starfish Arms

Starfish are ocean animals.

There are hundreds of kinds.

Starfish look like stars.

Most have five arms.

They have spiny skin.

Some starfish have

more arms.

A sun starfish can

have forty!

Tube feet help starfish move.

The tubes are like suction cups.

Starfish use their feet to crawl

along the ocean floor.

How do you think tubes help starfish move?

Bigger animals try to eat starfish.

They may tear off an arm.

But the starfish will grow

a new one.

Starfish are many sizes and colors.

This starfish is bright red. The color scares away bigger animals.

Why might bigger animals be afraid of bright colors?

Starfish have tiny eyes.

Each arm has an eye.

The eye is on the tip.

Why do you think starfish eyes are on the arms?

A starfish can open

a shell.

It pushes its

stomach inside.

It eats the animal

in the shell.

Then the starfish pulls

its stomach back

into its body.

Starfish lay eggs.

Baby starfish float in the water.

They will be adults in two years.

Parts of a Starfish

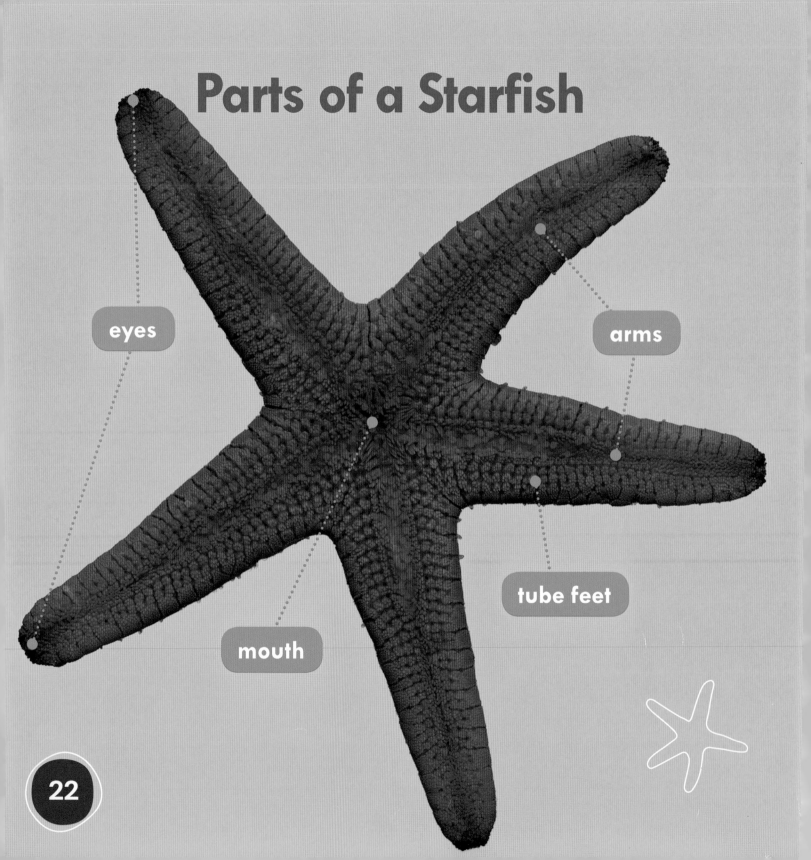

eyes

arms

tube feet

mouth

Picture Glossary

eggs

small, round objects that have babies inside

shell

a hard case that covers an animal

spiny

sharp and pointy

tube feet

small body parts that help a starfish move

Index

Read More

Gibbs, Maddie. *Sea Stars*. New York: PowerKids Press, 2014.

Meister, Cari. *Sea Stars*. Minneapolis: Bullfrog Books, 2013.

Metz, Lorijo. *Discovering Starfish*. New York: PowerKids Press, 2012.

Photo Credits

The images in this book are used with the permission of: © fenkieandreas/Shutterstock.com, p. 5; © Vilainecrevette/Shutterstock.com, pp. 6, 23 (bottom left); © Norbert Wu/ Minden Pictures/Newscom, pp. 8–9; © Jason Mintzer/Shutterstock.com, pp. 10, 23 (bottom right); © tiabri/Shutterstock.com, pp. 13, 14–15; © scubaluna/Shutterstock.com, p. 17; © towlake/iStock.com, pp. 18–19, 23 (top right); © ArtyAlison/iStock.com, pp. 21, 23 (top left); © JaysonPhotography/Shutterstock.com, p. 22. Front Cover: © jopelka/Shutterstock.com.